Put it on paper, speak it, burn it, share it,
lock it up, or send it back.
It's your choice just...

GET IT OUT

Write Your Way to Healing

Christel M. Hoydic

INTRODUCTION

I'm so proud you're here and ready to find YOU, the you that is NOT defined by your trauma. It is not easy, but I know from personal experience that digging deep and getting every last detail of your trauma out helps. You can move through this journal as quickly or as slowly as you'd like. I encourage you to take your time and deeply contemplate each prompt as you get to it. I created this journal to share my journey and hopefully inspire you to work through every page and every minute. CHEERS to growth & healing.

Before you begin, go to page 63 and dog ear that page. While you are completing this journal, you should refer back and document your nightmares if and when you have them. If you struggle with any of the prompts in this book, move to the next prompt and come back to it at another time. If you are feeling depressed, worse than at the start, frustrated, or want to quit, just remember it's going to get worse before it gets better. That's when the work is happening. I encourage you to be kind to yourself and Don't Give Up!

If you or someone you know may be struggling with suicidal thoughts, you can call the U.S. National Suicide Prevention Lifeline at 800-273-TALK (8255) any time day or night, or chat online. Crisis Text Line also provides free, 24/7, confidential support via text message to people in crisis when they dial 741741.

MY STORY

I chose to become a surrogate for a friend because I was going to create a family for someone who I thought was an amazing person. I was also going to be an "Aunt." Sadly, after the red dye on the pregnancy test changed, so did the person I thought I knew. Twenty-six is the number of traumas that occurred throughout those nine months. Twenty-six times I was brought to my knees in heartbreak. I was blamed for the death of one of the babies at twenty weeks (originally a twin pregnancy), I was degraded for the food I was eating, my ethics were questioned, and I was verbally abused. Would you believe I was called selfish? You wouldn't believe the stories I held inside during that entire year, including being assaulted at the delivery. I just kept thinking and praying that things would change. That he would change. That the original plan of being a village would hold true.

I was in survival mode; I disconnected and survived. My therapist compared what I went through to that of someone held captive in someone's basement--heck, similar to a handmaid. For two years it was a full-time job to make sense of the anxiety, depression, and PTSD that I was left with. I was an empty shell of my old self and I just wanted "me" back. I was working with my therapist, psychologist, EMDR specialist, Reiki master, a naturopath, podcasts, books... and the list goes on just trying to heal.

This journey has been incredibly hard. I was unable to listen to sad music, meditate, or do yoga. Babies and pregnant women were huge triggers. I avoided my friends whom I was "pregnant" with. My heart felt like it was beating out of my chest and I was just trying to breathe all day long. My meds were at their max. I had even gotten my medical marijuana card just to find something that would take the edge off--something to help me sleep without nightmares and face everyday problems without losing my mind.

I was broken both mentally and physically. I had insane guilt for the situations I had brought into my son's life, and for the longest time, I had felt I lost him between being pregnant, pumping, or just sad. There were times I wondered what was more emotionally damaging for him: to watch the shell of his mom not be able to do anything or if I wasn't here at all. While I love and appreciate what an incredible job my wife did at holding me together and supporting me in every way possible, I hate that she had to be that person.

I can go on and on, but the reason I am sharing my darkest days with you is that I finally felt the weight lifting off of my shoulders. I started smiling again, I started going full days without crying, and I even looked forward to leaving my house. This all happened when I *Got It Out*. When I told my story. From start to finish. Detail by detail, I shared my story. I found that telling my story helped me make sense of it all. It helped me to realize that it WAS very traumatic and it made me understand why I had these new diagnoses. It took the guilt I had for being depressed off of me and helped me see what happened with open eyes. It helped me to desensitize to the events a bit, and furthermore, it helped me to connect and find a way to feel good about what happened. I wish I had pushed through the pain of telling my story earlier. I wish I had looked through the emails, the texts, the recordings, and the videos, and made sense of the traumas earlier. I went from screaming "GET HIM OUT" in the delivery room as my abuser watched on to "GET IT OUT" as I found my voice. I hope you do, too. It might not be easy. In fact, it *IS* going to be hard. But, one prompt at a time, one day at a time, one week at a time, I hope that you find the same level of peace that I have. You can choose to do whatever you want with this journal when you are finished: keep it for yourself, share it with your family, send it back to me (exciting details about this option at the end of this journal), burn it, lock it up, throw it away. Whatever happens in the end, you will have gotten it all out and be on a better path to healing.

I sat in the corner of the couch wishing the pain away. Day after day, hour after hour, I wished it away. I thought that with each day that passed I would be further from the trauma and pain. Six weeks turned into twelve, then months, then years had passed. I stopped sharing my emotions publicly as I thought maybe I was stuck in sadness. I never talked about him or any of the things he did to me. So why was I still sad?! **How long has it been since your trauma occurred?** *Don't feel guilty about this time and repeat after me: THERE IS NO TIMELINE ON HEALING. Every single person is different. There is no right or wrong way to heal.*

_____
_____
_____
_____
_____
_____
_____
_____
_____
_____
_____
_____
_____

What has been stopping you from telling your story?

_____
_____
_____
_____
_____
_____
_____
_____
_____
_____
_____
_____
_____
_____

August 20, 2019. That's the date that my trauma came to a climax. After nine months of abuse. **What is the duration of time that your trauma continued on for?**

_____
_____
_____
_____
_____
_____
_____
_____
_____
_____
_____
_____
_____
_____
_____
_____
_____
_____

How often do you think back on your trauma?

_____
_____
_____
_____
_____
_____
_____
_____
_____
_____
_____
_____
_____
_____

I went back to work a little less than four months after the peak of my trauma. Going back to work was difficult, as I'm sure you can imagine. But not long after I started going was when the COVID pandemic hit the world. Teaching at a private school of students with special needs, I was sent home to Zoom with my students for what ended up being the following year. At the time, I thought this was good timing. I secretly celebrated that I could go back home, go back to my safe place and take more time to heal. Everyone agreed. Until the year turned into two and beyond. While there is no timeline for healing, mental health is so damn hard. I do believe, looking back this did put me into a longer funk than maybe I would have been if forced to face the world. **Was there anything in your timeline that got in the way of your healing?**

Anything that prolonged it?

Have you told anyone about your trauma? Like start to finish, front to back, part by part. Other than your therapist or anyone who has lived it along with you. Have you sat down and told anyone all of it? I didn't. I was so hopeful that things would change. I was willing to not stick up for myself and "move on", so throughout my trauma of 10 months I kept quiet during most of the abuse. For two years after, I thought by NOT talking about all the details (except to my therapist) that I would move on. I would forget about it. The trauma would just go away. I just needed to move on.

_____

_____

_____

_____

_____

_____

_____

_____

_____

What support do you need in order to tell your story?

_____

_____

_____

_____

_____

_____

_____

_____

_____

_____

_____

In what ways do you still have some healing to do?

_____

_____

_____

_____

_____

_____

_____

_____

_____

Why did it take so long to speak out?

My wife, my son, and my dog. During even the darkest times, they are the reason I am here. Whether it was their support and love, or knowing what it would do to them not being here anymore. I had no choice. I had to show my son I can recover from this. I had to show him that there will be shit in life and you may get knocked down a time or two, but there is no other choice but to keep pushing. I wanted to make my wife proud of me. It was hard. It is still really hard. But, I will keep pushing for them. **Who do you push for when you don't want to push for yourself?**

_____
_____
_____
_____
_____
_____
_____
_____

Create a list of 5 positive things in your life right now.

_____
_____
_____
_____
_____
_____
_____
_____
_____
_____

What are you in control of in this moment?

_____
_____
_____
_____
_____
_____
_____
_____

Prior to my trauma, I didn't quite understand anxiety. I would tell people with depression to just cheer up, and I will admit I thought panic attacks were dramatic. I wholeheartedly apologize for this ignorance and lack of empathy. I stand corrected and do not wish this on anyone. **Did you have an understanding and/or respect for mental illness prior to having it yourself?**

_____
_____
_____
_____
_____
_____
_____
_____
_____

Do any disorders run in your family?

_____
_____
_____
_____
_____

Do you know anyone close to you that suffers from any type of mental disorder?

_____
_____
_____
_____
_____

Do you have a person? Who is there for you no matter what?

_____
_____
_____
_____
_____
_____

Therapist, Psychologist, Reiki, Holistic Doctor, Naturopath, EMDR, DBT, and Heat therapy are just a few of the things that I tried in the two years that I struggled with my mental health. It was a full-time job. Each time I had to start from scratch and find a way to summarize my story, and each time I just wished I would magically be cured. I was committed to my mental health and it seems that was all I could focus on for those two years. **What have you tried or want to try thus far?**

_____
_____
_____
_____
_____
_____
_____
_____
_____

Have you ever gone to therapy? If so, is it helpful? If not, what is holding you back?

_____
_____
_____
_____
_____
_____
_____
_____
_____

What are 5 things that made you happy before your trauma? Are you able to find happiness in these people, place or things now? If not, what would make you feel happy right now?

_____
_____
_____
_____
_____
_____
_____
_____
_____

I am > I was. I got this tattooed on my finger. This is something that I am still wrapping my head around. The words that I had repeated to my therapist over and over again for years of therapy were, "I just want me back." She explained while I cried that I would never be "me" again. But that didn't mean the new me wasn't going to be better than the old me, that after going through everything I did there is no way I can be the same person. I had to let go of the old and find the new. Which is a process, but today I am > I was.

Who were you before your trauma?

_____
_____
_____
_____
_____
_____
_____

It made me sad to think about this person and know that I can never be the same after everything that happened. I had to process and mourn the old me to make room for the new me. **How does this make you feel?**

_____
_____
_____
_____
_____

Thinking about ways I can use my trauma to help others helped me to find some peace in the trauma. What are some ways you can turn your trauma into growth?

_____
_____
_____
_____
_____
_____
_____
_____
_____

After I accepted that I was working on the new me and needed to let go of the old, I started to look at who I AM in the present. Who I could be. How I could turn my trauma into something positive or helpful for others. I still didn't believe it and was still wrapping my head around I AM > I WAS. To this day, I am still working on the me that is greater than I was. I do believe I can get there. **Have you accepted that you can never be the same person you were before your trauma?**

_____
_____
_____
_____
_____
_____
_____
_____
_____
_____

Do you have any quotes, sayings, or memes that you find comfort in, use as inspiration, or repeat daily?

_____
_____
_____
_____
_____
_____
_____
_____

Without answering "the trauma," what is one thing you can change in your life now? What can you do to change it starting today?

_____
_____
_____
_____
_____
_____
_____
_____

I walked up to the pharmacy desk and without looking up told the woman who asked "Prescription for Hoydic?" She quickly located the Zoloft that the hospital prescribed and asked me to verify my address. The words wouldn't come out. I couldn't speak. I turned around to look for my wife who was finding other items on our lists in the aisles. My hands started to tremble and my heart was racing. "Are you ok, I just need your address?" the pharmacy staff asked. The tears streamed down my face. I opened my mouth, but nothing came out. I looked around and started walking away from the desk, then finally felt relief at that moment as my wife came into view. "JEN" I was able to yell her name. It was at that moment that I realized this is larger than I thought. I was not ok and I did need that Zoloft that I was there to pick up. **Did you have an "oh, shit" moment? A day, a week, an incident, or a time that you realized you were at the beginning of an emotional journey deeper than one you've ever experienced? Write about that moment.**

_____
_____
_____
_____
_____
_____
_____
_____
_____
_____
_____
_____
_____
_____

What was the specific thing you recognized in that moment?

_____
_____
_____
_____
_____
_____
_____
_____
_____

Have you told anyone about this moment (why or why not)?

_____
_____
_____
_____
_____
_____
_____
_____
_____
_____
_____
_____
_____
_____
_____
_____

Do you have a support person? If so, who?

_____
_____
_____
_____
_____
_____
_____
_____
_____
_____
_____
_____
_____
_____
_____

I remember driving to therapy a few days later. This was the first time I left my house. I was alone in my quiet car as I drove through the main street. I was hyper-focused on a woman pushing her baby in a stroller who smiled as she walked down the street, a mother and her kids looking through the glass of the toy store laughing and pointing at the stuffed animals in the windows, a gorgeous woman in her business suit perfectly put together and her curls bouncing as she walked across the street to get her coffee. Everyone was living their life. Life was moving all around me. Everyone was happy. I felt like I was there, but no one could see me. It felt like life was moving all around me, but my life had stopped. I felt like this was all a movie set that I accidentally stumbled onto. I waited for the director to yell "CUT."

Was there a time that you were not as present as you would have liked to be?

_____
_____
_____
_____
_____
_____
_____
_____

What specific emotions did you feel during these moments as you looked around?

_____
_____
_____
_____
_____

Was there a certain person or thing that you wished you could do or be?

_____
_____
_____
_____
_____
_____
_____
_____

For two years I avoided social situations at every chance I could get, for many reasons. One was that I didn't want anyone to see my body. I have a postpartum body with no baby to show for it. I felt like everyone was going to look at me, question my weight, feel bad for me, or silently judge me. I wished I could wear a shirt that said, "I was just abused as a surrogate for my ex-friend." **Was there a time you avoided situations? What would your shirt say?**

_____
_____
_____
_____
_____
_____
_____
_____
_____
_____

Body image issues were something I struggled with as a child, but didn't realize the effects until the trauma brought them up. Is there something from your childhood that your trauma brought up?

_____
_____
_____
_____
_____
_____
_____
_____

What is your greatest fear right now?

_____
_____
_____
_____
_____
_____
_____
_____
_____

I care what other people think of me. I care way too much. This is something that my wife is always reminding me that I need to let go of. It shouldn't matter AT all. But it does. Sharing my story and putting myself out there was really putting me in a vulnerable position. Allowing comments, judgments, and more. I didn't want to share about when I decided to pump because people would shake their heads and roll their eyes at my vulnerability. There were other parts I felt like others wouldn't agree with me so it scared me to share. **What part of your story are you avoiding the most for fear of judgment?**

_____
_____
_____
_____
_____
_____
_____

Are you scared of what other people will think when hearing your story?

_____
_____
_____
_____
_____
_____
_____
_____
_____

Being gentle on yourself is something that took a while to learn to do, and still do. What are ways you can show yourself love and build up your confidence?

_____
_____
_____
_____
_____
_____
_____

There were always specific parts of the trauma that I relived over and over again. Often all day long I couldn't shake it. I remember the sights, the sounds, and every single second. "We are going to bring him in now," they said. I remember holding on to the rail, looking at my wife. I remember what she was wearing, and I remember the smell of the nurse who distracted me from seeing him. I can write for days about all the details of this most traumatic moment. **Is there a part of your trauma that you relive or re-experience over and over again? Write about everything you remember from that specific memory.**

_____
_____
_____
_____
_____
_____
_____
_____
_____
_____
_____
_____
_____
_____
_____
_____
_____
_____
_____
_____
_____

How did you feel in those moments?

_____
_____
_____
_____
_____
_____
_____
_____

On the flip side of that, there were many parts of the story that I didn't remember at all or as vividly. Parts that, until I started telling my story, looking at texts, digging through emails, and listening to voice recordings I had totally pushed out of my mind. In revisiting these features, I realized that these times were very traumatic. These were important moments that helped to explain the state of my mental health. But, at the time, my body and mind were doing all they can do to protect me from pure overload. **Do you have a hard time remembering certain parts?**

_____
_____
_____
_____
_____
_____
_____
_____
_____
_____
_____
_____
_____
_____
_____

Do you have a person, a recording, text messages, or any other way that you can revisit the trauma and reveal these details?

_____
_____
_____
_____
_____
_____
_____
_____
_____
_____
_____
_____
_____
_____

On the flip side of that, there were many parts of the story that I didn't remember at all or as vividly. Parts that, until I started telling my story, looking at texts, digging through emails, and listening to voice recordings I had totally pushed out of my mind. In revisiting these features, I realized that these times were very traumatic. These were important moments that helped to explain the state of my mental health. But, at the time, my body and mind were doing all they can do to protect me from pure overload. **Do you have a hard time remembering certain parts?**

_____
_____
_____
_____
_____
_____
_____
_____
_____
_____
_____
_____
_____

Do you have a person, a recording, text messages, or any other way that you can revisit the trauma and reveal these details?

_____
_____
_____
_____
_____
_____
_____
_____
_____
_____
_____
_____

The list of things that triggered me started to grow. Some obvious like pregnant women and babies. But other triggers throughout the day brought up emotions that were sometimes deeper than I could even wrap my head around: men cheering at a basketball game, men in general, heck even Oreos. Some made sense, but some things on my list I still don't understand. **What things trigger an emotion in you?**

_____
_____
_____
_____
_____
_____
_____
_____
_____
_____
_____

Describe in detail how you feel when you are "triggered"?

_____
_____
_____
_____
_____
_____
_____
_____
_____
_____

How long do you find yourself in turmoil when presented with a trigger?

_____
_____
_____
_____
_____
_____
_____
_____

At the beginning of my healing journey, I didn't even know I was on a journey. I just thought I would eventually wake up and feel better. But I quickly learned this was going to take work. While everything made me cry--literally--there were some things that made me cry the most. **What makes you cry the most?**

_____
_____
_____
_____
_____
_____
_____
_____
_____
_____
_____
_____

Have you ever cried without knowing why?

_____
_____
_____
_____
_____
_____
_____
_____
_____
_____

Do you let yourself cry when you need to?

_____
_____
_____
_____
_____
_____
_____
_____

For two years I didn't give my trauma the weight it deserved. Even though my therapist told me over and over again how she could relate what I went through to a war veteran, to someone who was held captive in a basement, or even to a handmaid, I didn't give these words any weight. She said "profound trauma" over and over and over again. And, while I felt the emotions of profound trauma, I didn't quite buy it. It wasn't until I started sharing my entire story and got the same reaction. Not saying in any way that what others feel or think makes a trauma valid; it just helped me open my eyes and start to treat my mental health with the intensity it deserved. Once I realized that my trauma was really traumatic, I was better able to attack my healing process. I no longer shook off her words, I embraced them. **Do *you* believe your trauma is valid? Why or why not? If not, what is stopping you from embracing your trauma?**

_____

_____

_____

_____

_____

_____

_____

_____

_____

Do you think of yourself as a victim?

_____

_____

_____

_____

_____

Has anyone tried validating your trauma and you didn't "believe" them?

_____

_____

_____

_____

_____

_____

_____

The more I looked at, talked about, and dissected my current trauma and all of the parts, the more I saw how things from my childhood affected my mental health. Now, this is not to say that without the past I wouldn't have been affected because what happened was *NOT* ok and would not be ok for *ANYONE*. But there are reasons I can now see why certain parts hurt maybe a little more. For example, after I miscarried one of the twins, he tried to blame me for this loss. He questioned my exercise, my diet, and my every action. When he was shot down by doctor after doctor, he then decided on his own accord at twenty-five weeks pregnant he wanted me to be on a specific diet. He told me this in a text after he had already degraded the way he assumed I was eating. This text raised my heart rate and my blood pressure, and my entire body tensed up. I couldn't breathe. Looking back at this I can relate this to my childhood, teenage years, and adulthood as I struggled with weight my entire life. Although "struggle" is a funny word because I thought I was HUGE; my nickname was "porky" and I was constantly asked "Do you really need that?" when I reached for a snack. Looking back, my prom dress was a size 6. Gosh, I wish I could still be that "porky." I wish I wasn't even thinking about my weight right now! **Did your trauma bring to light any previous incidents that maybe you didn't remember until now?**

_____
_____
_____
_____
_____
_____
_____
_____
_____
_____
_____
_____
_____
_____
_____
_____
_____
_____
_____

I have regrets. If I could turn back the hands of time there are many things I would change. Knowing that none of this is my fault, there was nothing I could do to change what happened, and that I went into it with love and all good intention. I still wish I could turn back the hands of time. Starting with the obvious, I would say "No, I will not carry your babies," but even after that, had I still said yes, there are other things throughout that I would change. **If you could go back, what would you change?**

_____
_____
_____
_____
_____
_____
_____
_____
_____

Do you blame yourself for the things that happened to you?

_____
_____
_____
_____
_____
_____
_____
_____
_____

Is there anything you feel you need to forgive yourself for?

_____
_____
_____
_____
_____
_____
_____

I thought I was dying. Like literally dying. I wrote letters to my loved ones and was recording messages to my son. Every day my heart would race and I swore I was going to drop dead of a heart attack at any point in my house. I was so tired I swore I had Mono, Lyme disease, or some acute heart failure. I was short of breath, used my inhaler at least 10 times a day, and thought my lungs were going to collapse at any moment. I took Tylenol daily for my headaches. I even once thought I had a brain tumor. I called my doctor A LOT. I went for blood work all the time. Each and every time after receiving negative tests I would remind myself that I have anxiety. But in those moments I couldn't think of anything except dying. There was no way anxiety can make me feel this awful for so long. **Have you experienced anything like this? Did your mental health symptoms ever scare you?**

During the lowest of my lows, I had some really dark thoughts. I was constantly weighing the pros and cons of life. My son was my main source of concern. Was I causing more harm to my son and his future mental health to watch me struggle so badly? It wasn't fair to him that all I did was cry, that I didn't want to get off the couch, that I didn't want to leave the house, that I was short-tempered and not even a sliver of the mom that I used to be. Would it be easier for him if I wasn't there at all? I convinced myself of the latter and definitely had a few really dark moments. A few days that I thought were going to be the end, there seemed to be no light at the end of the tunnel during that time. I needed out of my own head. BUT I leaned on my wife, my son, my dog, my therapist, and my community. I realized that I would show him strength, I would show him healing, and I would fight every day to show him that there is a way out. Writing about this time is hard. It definitely makes me want to cry; it is also very triggering still, but I think the honesty and admittance of it are important for me, my son, and my future.

What (if any) are some dark feelings that you might be holding on to?

_____
_____
_____
_____
_____
_____
_____
_____
_____
_____
_____

Do you feel as if you are stronger than you were then now?

_____
_____
_____
_____
_____
_____
_____
_____
_____

Every time I would talk to my therapist we talked about the fact my story was so unique that it was hard to find a "support group." I felt so alone and just wanted someone to understand me, to "sit" with me. It wasn't until I started sharing my story did I realize that there were so many parts of my story that many could relate to. Miscarriage, sexual assault, verbal abuse, and narcissism, to name a few. **Do you think anyone will be able to relate to your story? If so, what kind of person?**

_____
_____
_____
_____
_____
_____
_____
_____
_____
_____
_____
_____
_____
_____
_____

Are you a part of a support group? If so, what kind? If not, what has stopped you?

_____
_____
_____
_____
_____
_____
_____
_____
_____
_____
_____
_____
_____
_____
_____

HOW ARE YOU FEELING? I remember this question was so incredibly difficult. The question alone would make me cry. I found myself avoiding any interactions where this question would be asked, which is literally the first question in social interactions 101. Take a second and genuinely answer full of thought. **How are you feeling??**

_____
_____
_____
_____
_____
_____
_____
_____
_____
_____

What is the response you typically tell people when they ask?

_____
_____
_____
_____
_____
_____
_____
_____
_____

What response do you look forward to answering?

_____
_____
_____
_____
_____
_____
_____
_____

SELF LOVE

I hated everything about myself. My body, my weight, my hair, my clothes. I went from not leaving the house without curling my hair and my lashes in the perfect place to not leaving the house at all. Not doing my hair, never wearing makeup, and living in oversized sweatshirts. I didn't want anyone to see me; heck I didn't even want to look at myself in the mirror. For a long time, I didn't realize how bad this was until my therapist really pushed and asked me for an *I AM* statement. I was unable to ever answer an *I AM* ___ with actual feelings. I am a mom, I am a woman; you know, the obvious factual answers I could do, but nothing beyond that. I tried. I tried so many times.

Everyone says "be kind to yourself," but the more I tried, the harder it felt and the longer I cried. For me, all I could do was focus on the fact that I couldn't say these things. It made it worse. I was so focused on making it better that I made it worse. In fact, I realized when I started telling my story that there was no way I could have healed my self-esteem when I was still stuck with so much trauma. Once I started telling my story, I let go of focusing on my looks. Somehow, as the weight of the story left, my care for myself grew without even knowing, and without a second thought one day I put on makeup. I realized "Holy crap--I care." I looked at a TikTok of myself and loved the way my eyes looked, then complimented myself without even thinking. It's still a work in process, but I realize the more I let go the more I like about myself.

What negative things did this make you think about yourself?

Do you have any self-care activities in place? If not, what could you add to your journey?

_____
_____
_____
_____
_____
_____
_____
_____
_____
_____
_____
_____
_____
_____
_____
_____
_____
_____
_____
_____
_____
_____
_____
_____
_____
_____
_____
_____
_____
_____
_____
_____
_____

How would you describe yourself now? Right now, at this moment. Dig deep.
Who are you?

_____
_____
_____
_____
_____
_____
_____
_____
_____
_____
_____
_____
_____
_____
_____
_____
_____
_____
_____
_____
_____
_____
_____
_____
_____
_____
_____
_____
_____
_____
_____
_____

Who do you want to be? It is so important to me to work through this trauma so that I can be the best mom, an amazing wife, and an inspiration to others who have felt such deep pain. I want to come out on top. Stronger, then ever. I don't want people to look at me and say "poor thing", "it ruined her", or "never came back from it." I want to be happy. I want to be a badass. I want to be an inspiration. *I want to be me.*

What makes you smile?

_____
_____
_____
_____
_____
_____
_____
_____
_____
_____
_____

In what ways do you still have healing to do?

_____
_____
_____
_____
_____
_____
_____
_____
_____
_____
_____
_____
_____
_____
_____
_____
_____
_____
_____
_____

It sounds cliché, but how could you turn these lemons into lemonade? I found that sharing my story started out selfishly as a way for me to "get it out." In turn, I was helping so many others who were holding it in, who had similar stories, and who could connect to me in the smallest way or the biggest. It kept me going, kept me pushing, and helped others, too (don't forget sharing your story is a choice with getting it out). **If sharing your story were to help someone else, whom do you envision this person to be?**

_____
_____
_____
_____
_____
_____
_____
_____
_____
_____
_____
_____
_____
_____
_____
_____
_____
_____
_____
_____
_____
_____
_____
_____
_____
_____
_____

I always give the best advice. I NEVER used to listen to my own advice. I am currently working on getting better at this. With the help of my therapist, I asked myself what I would tell another person in my position. At the darkest of times, the result was the complete opposite of the way I was talking to myself, of the actions I was taking, or the plans I had going forward. I shared this advice with and helped others. Which in turn helped me. Seeing the words on paper, I couldn't justify not trying to follow even just a little of it. So whether you already have the advice from your experiences or you are talking to a "friend": **What advice would you give to others in your situation?**

Will you or have you followed this advice?

_____
_____
_____
_____
_____
_____
_____
_____
_____
_____
_____
_____
_____
_____
_____
_____
_____
_____
_____

What is/was holding you back?

_____
_____
_____
_____
_____
_____
_____
_____
_____
_____
_____
_____
_____

When thinking about my trauma the thoughts and memories were fragmented, even the most climatic part that I truly believe was the breaking point of what was to come for my mental health. The assault I endured while giving birth while "he" watched as I screamed for the staff to get him out, while they all redirected my screams and ignored my wishes. This was the moment I wish I could erase. The bad memory I swear I would have been easier able to move on without. And for so long, I did everything I could to distract myself from thinking about this time. I tried really hard not to talk about it, not to think about, or dwell on it. Until I did, over and over and over again. In the end, what helped was to relive this moment. It's not going to be easy. It may be ugly. I promise each time you do this it will get easier. You will notice different things about that moment. You will find yourself desensitizing to it. You might even find some good. You may have more than one moment. Take one event within your trauma at a time. But dissecting this moment, focusing on it, and writing about it a few times will help you to both desensitize yourself to this trauma as well as open your eyes to different parts you may have locked away, other emotions you may not even realize you are or had felt and maybe even some positivity. **What traumatic event do you feel has the most profound impact on your mental health?**

_____
_____
_____
_____
_____
_____
_____
_____
_____
_____
_____
_____
_____
_____
_____
_____
_____
_____
_____

When thinking about this moment, what emotion comes to mind?

_____
_____
_____
_____
_____
_____
_____
_____
_____
_____
_____
_____
_____
_____

How does this moment make you feel about yourself? What would others say about you at this moment?

_____
_____
_____
_____
_____
_____
_____
_____
_____
_____
_____
_____
_____
_____
_____
_____
_____
_____

The next five pages should be done on the same day; be sure you have enough time before you begin. Now I want you to close your eyes and really picture that moment. Put yourself back. Notice every little detail. You might cry. You might want to stop. You might want to run. But I know you can do it. **Set a timer for two minutes and just think about that time. When the timer goes off, write. Write everything that comes to mind. Even if it doesn't make sense at this moment. Write about anything and everything you notice when thinking about that memory.**

_____
_____
_____
_____
_____
_____
_____
_____
_____
_____
_____
_____
_____
_____
_____
_____
_____
_____
_____
_____
_____
_____
_____
_____
_____
_____
_____
_____
_____

And again. Set your timer. Take a deep breath and visualize that moment.

_____
_____
_____
_____
_____
_____
_____
_____
_____
_____
_____
_____
_____
_____
_____
_____
_____
_____
_____
_____
_____
_____
_____
_____
_____
_____
_____
_____
_____
_____
_____
_____
_____
_____

And again. Set your timer. Take a deep breath and visualize that moment.

_____
_____
_____
_____
_____
_____
_____
_____
_____
_____
_____
_____
_____
_____
_____
_____
_____
_____
_____
_____
_____
_____
_____
_____
_____
_____
_____
_____
_____
_____
_____

And again. Set your timer. Take a deep breath and visualize that moment.

_____
_____
_____
_____
_____
_____
_____
_____
_____
_____
_____
_____
_____
_____
_____
_____
_____
_____
_____
_____
_____
_____
_____
_____
_____
_____
_____
_____
_____
_____
_____
_____
_____
_____

And again. Set your timer. Take a deep breath and visualize that moment.

_____

_____

_____

_____

_____

_____

_____

_____

_____

_____

_____

_____

_____

_____

_____

_____

_____

_____

_____

_____

_____

_____

_____

_____

_____

_____

_____

_____

_____

_____

_____

_____

The next five pages should be done on the same day; be sure you have enough time before you begin. Do not skip a step. Do not shorthand. Do not cheat. Ideally, you would complete this once a week. All five prompts are to be filled out at the same moment. The same trauma, the same thought. **Set your timer. Take a deep breath and visualize that moment.**

And again. Set your timer. Take a deep breath and visualize that moment.

_____

_____

_____

_____

_____

_____

_____

_____

_____

_____

_____

_____

_____

_____

_____

_____

_____

_____

_____

_____

_____

_____

_____

_____

_____

_____

_____

_____

_____

And again. Set your timer. Take a deep breath and visualize that moment.

_____
_____
_____
_____
_____
_____
_____
_____
_____
_____
_____
_____
_____
_____
_____
_____
_____
_____
_____
_____
_____
_____
_____
_____
_____
_____
_____
_____
_____
_____
_____
_____
_____
_____

And again. Set your timer. Take a deep breath and visualize that moment.

_____

_____

_____

_____

_____

_____

_____

_____

_____

_____

_____

_____

_____

_____

_____

_____

_____

_____

_____

_____

_____

_____

_____

_____

_____

_____

_____

_____

_____

_____

_____

_____

_____

And again. Set your timer. Take a deep breath and visualize that moment.

_____
_____
_____
_____
_____
_____
_____
_____
_____
_____
_____
_____
_____
_____
_____
_____
_____
_____
_____
_____
_____
_____
_____
_____
_____
_____
_____
_____
_____
_____
_____

I encourage you to continue this exercise anytime you feel it necessary!

Forgiveness. I hate this one. Everyone will tell you that in order to heal you have to forgive. Over and over and over again. I have thought about this a lot during the past three years. I have tried to look at this from every angle possible. I was stuck on this for a while and convinced myself that I was a bad person for not being able to forgive. I am not that person. I don't forgive him. There is no way you can look at it. He is not forgiven, and not to mention he hasn't apologized. For me, forgiveness gives him a pass. Maybe this is a religious thing (which I'm not very); maybe this is something for someone bigger than me--heck this sounds like something a narcissist would say. But, I am ok with not understanding this concept. I don't have to be that person. *I no longer subscribe to what others' healing looks like for me*. This doesn't fit into my journey and only made it harder for some time because I couldn't understand this concept for my growth. I do not forgive you. **How do you feel about forgiveness?**

_____
_____
_____
_____
_____
_____
_____
_____
_____
_____
_____

Are you able to forgive your abuser?

_____
_____
_____
_____
_____
_____
_____
_____
_____
_____
_____
_____
_____

This led me to a message to Rob. Rob is the asshole, man, dude, *person* I had a baby for. Rob, whom I had no intention of ever seeing again, but hold so much anger towards for all the things I kept inside. For all the words I never said. I wanted so badly to just punch him in the face. But I knew even if I had the chance I wasn't emotionally strong enough to look him in the face without my fear and anxiety taking over. BUT I hate him so much. I have so much to say. This is something I worked hard to differentiate. I didn't want to forgive him, BUT I didn't want to hate him either. Hate and anger took up way too much space in my healing. So I wrote him a letter. I told him in that letter the things I needed to say. The words that I held in for so long, the swears and bad wishes I wanted to scream in his face. I wrote and wrote and didn't look back. I just wrote and then I burned that paper. I burned it in a fire pit. I literally got it out. And I let that shit go. It sounds so hokey, but it worked. It helped the hate to just be. My feelings didn't change per-say. But the anger, rage, and space he took up in my head burned away. Now it's your turn.
Write a letter to your abuser.

_____

_____

_____

_____

_____

_____

_____

_____

_____

_____

_____

_____

_____

_____

_____

_____

_____

_____

_____

_____

_____

_____

NOW its time to burn this letter and literally *GET IT OUT*.

NIGHTMARES – To this day I am still trying to find a way to heal my mind at night. I can say they have finally expanded to other things and not just my trauma but, nightmares is something that has affected me in a big way. One thing I wish I did earlier on was to write down some of the reoccurring nightmares or ones that affected me the most. I want this to be something you think about too. Sometimes paying attention to these nighttime thoughts can help you to really uncover parts that are most hurtful without even knowing it. **During the time it takes to complete this journal, dog-ear this page and keep referring back and writing things below when they occur. Although I hope that the next few pages remain empty for you.**

NIGHTMARES

NIGHTMARES

NIGHTMARES

NIGHTMARES

NIGHTMARES

NIGHTMARES

NIGHTMARES

Looking through pictures, text, and email, while hard, was helpful for me to put together the pieces and recognize my story as a whole, remember pivotal moments, and connect the dots. **Do you have anything that you can gather that will help you to tell your story?**

Before telling your story let's make a list of tools that can help you in dealing with the feelings that it may bring up. Do not avoid these feelings, but know that you can go at your own pace. As long as you have your "toolbox" ready and waiting. Some of the things that helped me the most were a weighted blanket, ice packs (that I used on my chest), ice baths for my face, exercise, breath-work, body scan, and 5 steps. **What tools do you have in your toolbox?**

_____
_____
_____
_____
_____
_____
_____
_____
_____
_____

Look around your house. What makes you smile?

_____
_____
_____
_____
_____
_____
_____
_____
_____

What is your favorite place to go that is local?

_____
_____
_____
_____
_____
_____
_____
_____
_____

YOUR STORY

Now it's time to write your story. Gather the things you may need, talk to the people who can fill in the gaps, and just write.

But here is the thing: I need you to set a timer for eleven minutes. Eleven minutes at a time. Eleven minutes a day, eleven minutes a week. Whatever pace you need to go at. But eleven minutes is just enough time to write a significant part of your story without overwhelming yourself either. Close the book and walk away giving yourself the time that is needed to digest. The time to process, accept, and heal.

When you are ready you will know. When you are ready you will open your journal, and start your next eleven minutes.

Now write your way to healing.

Your trauma does not define you.

_____
_____
_____
_____
_____
_____
_____
_____
_____
_____
_____
_____
_____
_____
_____
_____
_____
_____
_____
_____
_____
_____
_____
_____
_____
_____

It's a marathon, not a sprint.

There is no timeline on healing.

I am not alone.

I can handle this.

I AM > I WAS

I am allowed to struggle.

Be stronger than your excuses.

Get out of your own way.

I own my story.

I will not Give Up.

Recovery is the best revenge.

I am allowed to say no.

I am strong.

My feelings ARE valid.

I am doing the best I can.

I am worthy.

I will not quit.

I will ask for help.

Good things take time.

I believe in myself

Be the badass I AM!

I am incredible.

I am NOT my mental illness.

_____
_____
_____
_____
_____
_____
_____
_____
_____
_____
_____
_____
_____
_____
_____
_____
_____
_____
_____
_____
_____
_____
_____
_____
_____
_____

I am capable of amazing things.

Now that you have finished writing all of the details of your story, I pray that you feel a weight lifted and a true sense of healing. It is entirely up to you what you do with your journal. You can keep it on a shelf, lock it in a safe, burn it in a fire pit and watch the story disappear... it's entirely up to you but, let me add an option:

SEND IT BACK

With this option, you can do just that. You can choose to mail your journal (or a copy of it) back to me. Your story will be used on our *GET IT OUT* podcast, continuing to help you to get your trauma out. All stories will be anonymous and I will be sure to change names, locations, and likenesses. By sharing your story, it is my hope that you will find even further healing, as well as help others. Listeners may find a connection with you and they might be inspired by you. It could even give them the push they need to tell their story, get help, and keep pushing. I will have a yearly Book Burning Ceremony live on social media platforms. And who knows what the future will bring... a burning meetup?!?! Be sure to sign up at www.gethimoutt.com to get all the details of our book, podcast, and so much more to come.

Christel wants to live in a world where everyone is kind to one another. She was often found giving to others rather than herself, which led her to the experience she writes about here.

Over the years she wore many hats. Her most proud accomplishment is being a Mom and wife, but also included becoming a publisher and editor of a record breaking local newsletter and website for kids and families, connecting and giving to her community, 18 years of teaching social skills to children on the autistic spectrum - many of whom hold a special place in her heart still. She continued as a successful entrepreneur where the most important part was the connections she made with her community both near and far. She has received high praise for finding her voice and telling her trauma on TikTok's "Get Him Out", which helped her find healing, her village and her why!

When she's not connecting and helping thousands of women to feel strong, and boosting everyone else's confidence, she's hanging with her amazing wife, caring son and her doodle babies.

Enjoyed the journal and want more from this author?

Her First book *Get him out* is due to hit the shelves in December of 2022!

Join the village, connect with her and learn more at:

www.gethimoutt.com
gethimoutt@gmail.com
Tik-Tok: @gethimoutt
Instagram: @shop_smarties
Facebook Group: www.shopsmarties.com
Send It Back:
P.O. BOX 470
Middletown, CT 06457

If you or someone you know may be struggling with suicidal thoughts, you can call the U.S. National Suicide Prevention Lifeline at 800-273-TALK (8255) any time day or night, or chat online. Crisis Text Line also provides free, 24/7, confidential support via text message to people in crisis when they dial 741741.

rebel queen

With a combined 20+ years in publishing, we know how to help anyone write, launch, and market a book. So if a book is on your bucket list? We're the team to take it from brain dump to best seller.

RebelQueen.co
Facebook and Instagram @rebelqueenbooks

Made in United States
North Haven, CT
04 January 2023

30627044R00057